NOTEBOOK

RULED PAPER

THIS BOOK BELONGS TO:

authored by: Marcel Doll, Hammerschbüchel 10, 53797 Lohmar, Germany

Made in the USA
Monee, IL
13 December 2022

21392218R00069